SH:LAM

(The Doctor)

poems

JOSEPH A DANDURAND

MAWENZI
HOUSE

We acknowledge the support of the Canada Council for the Arts for our publishing program. We also acknowledge support from the Government of Ontario through the Ontario Arts Council.

Cover design by Sabrina Pignataro
Author photo: Peter Arkell

Library and Archives Canada Cataloguing in Publication

Title: Sh:lam = (the doctor) : poems / Joseph A Dandurand.
Other titles: Doctor
Names: Dandurand, Joseph A., author.
Identifiers: Canadiana (print) 2019008765X | Canadiana (ebook) 20190087722 | ISBN 9781988449715
   (softcover) | ISBN 9781988449722 (HTML) | ISBN 9781988449869 (PDF)
Classification: LCC PS8557.A523 S5 2019 | DDC C811/.54—dc23

Printed and bound in Canada by Coach House Printing

Mawenzi House Publishers Ltd.
39 Woburn Avenue (B)
Toronto, Ontario M5M 1K5
Canada
www.mawenzihouse.com

CONTENTS

Author's Note

The poems in this collection tell the truth of what has happened to my people. The Kwantlen people used to number in the thousands, but 80% of our people were wiped out by smallpox and now there are only 200 of us. The same fate was suffered by other river tribes in western Canada. As a Kwantlen man, father, fisherman, poet and playwright I believe the gift of words was given to me so I can tell our stories either upon stage or in a book of poetry or in our longhouses on cold winter nights.

The poems gathered here tell the tale of a Kwantlen man who has been given the gift of healing but also is a heroin addict living on the east side. It is my intent to share this story, a story that needs to be told.

What drove me to write these poems was the voice of the Healer, which came to me quickly, and it was with ease that each poem subsequently showed itself. To a writer these voices come so easily and without much pain only once in a while. I felt as though I was right there, either talking to a Sasquatch or crawling down an alley on the east side of Vancouver. It almost has a film quality to it, it's as if each poem were a scene from an epic tale.

As a simple humble man, it is with great pleasure that I share my words with anyone wishing to read my work. It is a book for you and I to reflect on and hope for all of us to find peace. This is a book of hope, loss, and redemption for all the poor souls who find themselves on the street and lost from where they truly come.

Doctor

I guess I am the same man
I was when I discovered who I am
and exactly what it is that I can do.
They, the people of the river,
had a word for me: Sh:Lam
and in English it meant: Doctor.
I remember centuries ago when
the river flowed just like it does today
there were a people who were burning
from the inside out
and they called it smallpox
but it was the most painful way
to see the other side
and I came from a cedar tree
where I had been listening
and crying as the children
of our river people began
to cough and I came and told
the people to give me fire
and I would eat the flames
and I did as the sickness
entered me and erupted
from the inside out
as flames burned the memories
of our all
of our illness
and I walked back and went up
to the top
of that cedar tree
and there I became again

a Sh:Lam
and I sat and I sat
for another century
as the world changed
and our people changed
and now I am here
in this city
in a place they call the Eastside
as the heroin
burns
our people
from
the inside
out.

The rain drops on her needle

We met in an alley
and at first we were lovers
as destiny had brought us
down from the mountains
where the old people
kept all the secrets.
The touch of her
the taste of her
the essence of her
covers me like an old
blanket once used in a
ceremony for all the forgiveness
as the old people
open their mouths
to form the word
"peaceful."
We were alive
in an alley
making love everywhere
but we always had a bottle
of cheap cooking wine
and the sourness
of it always on our breath
as we traded tongues
as we traded stories
as we tried to devour the
other as the west coast rains
fell hard on to the streets
of this treacherous place
and when I entered her

she would look into my eyes
and seek the word "peaceful"
but I had not been able
to speak my language
in a long time
and later in the darkness
of the night she would
sell herself for a taste
of the dragons and evils
that came to her
so easily
and she would heat
the poison
and jam the needle
into a vein
and she would disappear
as the rain drops fell on to
her needle
and she would
close her eyes
and open her mouth
searching for that word
we
now
know
is
"peaceful."

Born to walk and become

As a sh:lam I can change
and today I am a salmon egg
settling on the rocks
of the stream up river
and as I begin my parents die
and float above me in a dance
of death in a current that has
been here long before
the outside
came in.
As I grow I rush away
down river and begin the
feast of four years and I
enter the great ocean
where the bottom
is endless
and I eat and I gorge
on the life that gives
me life and I become
a great being but my body
aches for my beginning
and I enter back into
the river
that gave me life and I swim
and swim until
I cannot swim no more
and I explode my eggs
as a man comes and spreads
his seed on a million eggs
and then I walk out of the water

and I am naked
for all to see and I have become
the perfect form of a human
that has eaten for four years
and I enter the forest
as I slowly become
as I slowly become
yes
I
become
you.

The shine brings you home

I have changed and find myself
on a highway wetted with the
tears of our lost.
I am here to meet the man
who has taken all the women
and has put them
on the side of the road
in a puddle
by a tree
in a ditch
or slowly floating
to the bottom
of a creek.
I get a ride and I remember
the truck in every detail
and the smells of the dead
encircle this man as he
smokes and opens his window
he never looks at me.
I do not see fear or sorrow
from this man and he is
not from here
so he says
and he tells me of his family
his children
and the cost
of gasoline.
I look at him as he
appears to be on fire
and the heat of him

begins to burn my fingers
as I reach out and touch him
and all he sees and has seen
evaporates into a hot mist
and falls out the window as he
blows smoke from his
cigarette out into the
world he has forsaken
and when I get out
of the truck he waves
a tattooed arm at me
as the medicine
I have given him
begins to carry into his blood
and all the women circle
around him and they cry
and they scream
and it is the screams
that envelope him
and he accepts
the disease I have given him
by the touch of my hand
I have erased him
as the women cry
and scream
and this opens
up the sky
as the
shine
brings
you
home.

Healers made of stone

The three of us appeared
from the sky over ten
thousand years ago.
I was a man they both were
very powerful women
and I do not think
they liked me much
as they would hold hands
and laugh when they would
make the ice disappear
and I would try and anger them
as I whispered the word: allow
and a river would appear
filled with fish.
They would always want
to compete with me
and our battles became legends
as every time that I won
they would be angry
and they would turn
a pebble into a mountain
and scoff at me and as they
finally left and went back
to the sky they said something
like they would be back when I had
flooded the earth with so
many rivers filled with fish.
It is lonely here
as I am the only
doctor fallen from

the sky and now in
a world so filled
with pain and despair
but I whisper the word: allow
and a sun shines in a blue sky
where healers fall and return
to a blue sky where a man
sits on top of the highest mountain
created by healers
too stubborn to allow me
the taste of victory
and I can still see them
as they went up
turning back to
stare at me
trying to
trying
trying to
turn me
to
stone.

The strangeness of each other

I find myself on a train
sent to a school far away
and there are others like me
brown skinned
and full of fear.
They say they will break
bread in the morning
as when we arrived
it was too late
to feed the hunger.
I remember bells
that were so loud
they caused my teeth
to chatter and it was then
the father took me
like he did all the boys
and he led me into a
bathroom stall and told me
to wipe myself
as he tore away
all that I knew
was pure.
Later on a bus
going nowhere
as I squirm in my seat
I am a man now
and the old man sitting
next to me is an old
retired priest
and it is only I who

recognizes him
as the birth mark
on his right cheek
gives him away
and as a sh:lam
I touch him on the
cheek and he smiles at me
as the power in my touch
stops his heart
in one beat
and I get off the bus
and walk out into a day
like all days
where pureness
shadows the evil
of a priest who
has touched for the last time
as I said to him:
in the name of the father
the son
the holy ghost.

I populate

On a Six Nation in the
cold of a long winter
we are on her bed
and she is on top of me
saving me from my demons
she throws her head back
and I am taken to her world
for only a moment and I
release all of my gifts to her
and our child.
Across a bridge this
mighty warrior girl who
survived the war
takes me by the hand
and leads me into a forest
that has been saved for
centuries and we make love
standing up but she is ever
ready to run at the first
sight of a soldier
from across the bridge
and we release
our demons together
and later our child
rises up and takes the
gun and repeats.
In a city
not our own
we play quietly in
her room as her mother

sits in the other room
sipping tea as rain soaks
the west coast
as this girl and I
entwine ourselves
like snakes and we join
together in the glory
of our survival
as the rains soak us
until we no longer
need the other
and I walk away as her
body shakes and
receives the child
that will become a powerful
woman who destroys the evil
of men in a city
not our own.
Once I met a woman who
like me had spent time
in prison for murder
and she was wasted
in her own way and
so was I and it was another
cold day
in another cold city
and she became a demon
and we joined twisted tails
and it was I that became the
prisoner and she took from me
and took from me and she left
never to be seen again
but later a young man

came up to me in the street
and hugged me
and said goodbye.
By a cedar tree
we danced all night
and then I took her
and she took me
and the tree grew
to live a thousand years
and it gave the earth life
over and over again
and when I fell asleep
I awoke decades later
alone and I stood up
and walked for weeks
following a river made
by a sh:lam and I dove
in cleansing myself
of the love and the torture
of love as an eagle
came and hugged me
and the eagle whispered
goodbye
and the echo of that word
echoed into a cedar tree
put there
a century ago
by the
women
of
the
world.

The liquid of fate

Today I am the coyote
walking down a path that
used to be used for travel
between two different
river Indians and they would
go back and forth trading
items that both were
masters at creating.
At the end of the path
I come to an airport
and I get on a plane
heading east and halfway
there I jump out and become
the raven and I glide with
such beauty through the clouds
of some heaven.
Later at night I land
and turn into a human
and walk into the city
and all the lights turn
into stars in the clear
of night as I pick up a pipe
but it is not scared
no
it is made of glass
and I inhale the
pleasure and exhale
the pain out into the city
as the creatures come
alive.

Even later I sit in a corner
of an Indian bar and sitting
beside me telling the same story
over and over again is a
Sasquatch who needs a shave
as he tells his story with his
one tooth gleaming in
the shadows of this seedy bar.
In the morning I have
transformed back into a butterfly
and I leave the east and head back
west over the mountains
over the oceans
over the masses
of the lost.
When I finally land
I am the coyote on a path
that seems familiar
and it is as though the footprints
fit perfectly into every
step I have taken and I am home
in my village and all the children
come to me and ask:
where did you go, Father?
I wait a moment and answer:
I
went
to
find
myself.

Last days of luck

They dig up dirt looking
for bones of Eastside women
as the November rains
pound the earth.
Where are they?
Who are they?
Why are they?
Questions of the day as the
world carries on into
another day of loss and
the men come and they ask:
Is it her?
on a darkly lit street corner
she stands and smokes
and listens to the evening
trying to remember her past
her family
her children
and she cries one tear
and it falls down her
bruised face as an old pick-up
pulls up and she gets in
as if she knew him
and she did
she knew him.
Later on a different corner
a sister walks and jumps
over the puddles
and she sings an old song
from somewhere up river

past the city
past the concrete
past the evil
and she remembers her home
and the taste of fish as she
licks her lips and sighs
as an old pick-up comes
and she gets in for that
final ride into paradise.
I am here now and ask
this man in the old pick-up
if he has seen my sister
and he says he has and she
went very quietly
and I take this man's hand
and I throw him over a tree
and he hangs there begging me
for forgiveness
and I do forgive him
as I slide my fishing knife
from his throat to his belly
and he falls into
the ground and becomes
dirt to be dug up
in history
of the forgotten
if
not
lost.

Light of you

Within the cedar forest
there are little people
and they collect all that the
world has lost.
In the sky there are
eagles and hawks who
carry the clouds across
the sunset and they throw
them into the waves
of the eternal sea.
As you walk through the
valleys they say there are
giant footprints of the
creature called Sasquatch
who has a never-ending
journey as he looks for a mate
so he can continue
the mystery of who
he really is.
In a church there are love birds
who pass around the last piece
of bread and they gossip
about this and that.
In a cave sleeps a great
bear and she is so beautiful
as she dreams about a garden
of berries and she dreams of eating
until her belly can take no more
and she dreams.
In a cedar box sit my bones

and the people place the box
at the top of a tree
and I have become again
a sh:lam and I step out
and fall to the clouds
thrown there and I dive
into the sea and I search
for the light of you
but you have already left
and I follow your giant footsteps
across the universe always
listening for your voice as the
eagles and the hawks throw
more clouds at me and I
begin to fade back to the
reality of this day and like
the beautiful bear I dream
and dream
as I search
for
the
light
of
you.

Warm hands

I knew quite a few healers
in my time when I could
just pick up and venture out
into the places that held
so much sorrow.
There was this one lady who
could heal all the wrongs
that would creep into your
house and she would enter
and saying a small prayer
to herself she would
find the pain and she would
chase it into a corner and
she would scoop it up
with the cups of her hands
and she would open the door
and she would throw the sorrow
into the winds of glory.
There was another fine lady
who could gather all the
poison in your body and she
would say a small prayer
and she would rub her hands
together and touch the poor soul
and all the poisons would be
trapped in the cups of her warm hands
and she would open the door and
throw all the poison into the dust
of an old dirt road.
I tried to heal like all the doctors

I had met and sometimes
it worked but most times
I would become so sick from
what I had pulled out of an
old man who had only days
left of this world
and I think I gave him
and all I have healed some sort
of peace as I rub my hands together
my warm hands that have taken so much
pain and sorrow from the people
and I cough and spit out the poison
trying my best to be a doctor
a sh:lam
and I do as the warmth of
my hands and the hands
of all the healers
of this world
join together
and they
touch me
and they
touch
me.

Enter the transparent

I am now a drunk living
on the streets of any city's
skid row.
With me are the characters from
any great novel and we sip
the whiskey bottle as if it is
the last object to touch
our lips and the characters
perform for me to the sounds
of any great symphony
and they dance ballet
leaping over the filth
and the mayhem.
I begin to write poems
on slips of welfare cheques
and dirty napkins and the
poems flow onward from a
broken pencil to the lines
of the gods who are here
to see the show.
In my twilight of being a drunk
I am too weak now to write
and some of the characters
have placed a plastic blanket
over me and later that night
I arise somewhat like Jesus did
as he danced across the filth
and when I leave I go
up into air and somewhere
along the way they gave me wings

and written on the wings
were all my poems
and as we came nearer to
the sun
I watched
my wings
my words
burn.

The chains of the eager

Over time I have met others
like me and they usually gathered
in a clearing and they always came
in groups of three and they would
fire at me right away to see
what kind of sh:lam I am
and I would turn
their fire into ice and I
would walk deeper into
the clearing and it was then I got
my first look at who
they truly were and I knew
they had come from the ocean
and they looked somewhat
awkward walking on solid ground
but that does not hinder their need
to take a piece of me with them
back to the bottom of the
ocean as I politely tell them
to leave as this world is sacred
and that the people living here
might see them as a threat and
that the people here came
from the sky and that they had
a very strong medicine that
would appear as a song
and then the water creatures
fired some more fire my way
and then I had enough and I turned
them into ice and they sat there

frozen for centuries as the
people of this land gave them
a name which meant
where ice and fire meet
and I walked on as the
chains of the eager
break apart and fall
and become oceans
filled with creatures
so wonderful
that they begin
to sing a new song
and it rises up
out of the water
again
breaking
the
chains
of
the
eager.

A potent shame

I loved a girl who once
took a bayonet from a soldier
as she protected her younger
sister from the power of man
and his vastly wrong idea
of what peace really is.
I met another girl who
could drink me under
the table and as I hid
beneath all the tables
of all the bars she would
get up and dance the dance
of the devil and all the men
wanted her and at the end
of the night she would
pick me up and destroy me
as I dreamed of rolling waves
and silent trees that have
stood for so long they
have been forgotten.
In a place where the people
gather I sit across from a young
sh:lam and she knows
who she is and the powers
that she had over the simple
men and she would
look around the room
and find one man
and when their eyes met
he would begin to cry

and cry and all the other men
stood up and pounded drums
trying to save him but
he had gone to the other side
and as I looked across the room
her eyes met mine.
The last human I went with
gave me children who grew
up to become not like me
and they went to the
other side as I grew older
than the forgotten trees
who were still silent
and in this silence
I closed my eyes
searching for my next
opening in the sky
that will take me
to another time
and as the trees
stayed silent
I could hear the faint
cries coming from the
heavens and I recognized
those cries as they
were mine
and it was then
that I knew
I
would
become.

Pledge the depth

They gather
the abusers
the users
the deviant
and I lead them
to the edge of this place
and I tell them they
have a choice to jump
or be turned to stone.
A million stones sit
on the edge waiting
for the young
the pure
to come and skip
a stone across the
freedom.
I walked away in search
of all the true evil of this
place and I found him
and he told me that he had
been forgiven and that his
god understood
his desires
to destroy young minds
and I told him he had a choice
and as he jumped he looked
back to me and said:
I forgive you.
You see that from time to time
the evil and their belief that they

will live forever and they never
do and I walk on to another
edge of a place up river
from here and I again
gather all the abusers
and they stand there
looking over the edge
and they become stones
and they sit there as a
small child comes one day
and builds a wall of stones
and the wall sits there as the
edge of this place slowly
erodes to the wall and one
by one the stones fall
into the emptiness
of eternity
as the words:
I forgive you
fade
like
the
memory
of
an
abuser.

The slightest shadow

In the corner I see the images
of the entire history of this
planet and it's not good
but I told myself today
I would not dream the
emptiness of a needle
and that lasted about five minutes
and I am on the street
and I hustle and hustle
and I create enough for a piece
of some darkness.
We both lay there with
a needle hanging out of our arm
and outside the city burns
from too much love and lust
as the crows fly into
the backstreets picking away
at any human who was too slow
to move out of the way
and the crows pick them up
and carry them away
to the sanctuary and along
the way the crows drop them
into a cemetery
as their holes were
already dug
for them.
We both do not awake
from our last journey
and she is cold to the touch

and I too am cold
but I have been doing this
for a very long time
and I lift my head up
just in time as a screaming crow
nearly takes me away
and they take her up into
the love and the lust
of this city and I get up
and hustle and hustle
as the flame heats the
sweetness of my
passion and I close
my eyes as the needle
enters me like it has
for the past fifty years
and just one more
I say to myself
one more
movement
of the slightest shadow
as the
black
wings
surround
me.

Harmony with all of you

The task given to me when all
the ice had melted was to
welcome the sky people to
the river and to show them
how to fish and how to
build a fire to warm
themselves.
I moved on and came across
another doctor who did not like
the way I had created the sky
people and so this doctor
turned two of them into rocks
and he picked them up and threw
them into the sky and I
watched the rocks forever
as they never came back
down and the doctor told me
that with gifts comes
punishment for those
who do not listen.
In the past I have walked
into cities that have the
remnants of the sky people
and these poor beings
hang on to the dream of
one day returning home
but they have been punished
and abused by the world
they now live in and they
drink and drink
and smoke and smoke
until the rocks fall.

As I leave this time I
sometimes go into the forest
searching for the spirits
who are only known by
their myths and they become
carved masks and sit
on a wall in a place
that no longer knows
who they were.
And now I am back in the
sky and I look up and see
a rock coming right at me
and it passes through me
and I shudder and cry
as the rock turns into dust
that falls on the city
below and covers the sky people
as they fade to a page in a
history book about a once
great people who lived
on the river
and took fish and built
great fires to warm
the doctor who has now
turned himself
into a rock
and the sky people
throw him
into the river
never
to
see
him
again.

A true breath

There were times when all
I could do was to be alone
and I would walk to the
corner of this civilization
and I would stop and eat
a forbidden fruit as the
madness of what was really
going on in the world
and it was mostly unwinnable
wars raging of man vs man
and they topple over each other
and I could barely control
my sorrow for them for
they know not what they
have done.
The first bite of forbidden fruit
and the juices run down my
face to the earth
as up rises a child
of the purest pure
and the child begins to walk
and then runs past the flames
of some war and the child
grows wings and soars above
the carnage as fruit trees
become the dead
and with another taste
of the earth's gifts I get up
and move on to another time
and it is a time when there was

peace and all the children danced
and sang songs of freedom
and the animals came
in their disguises of a spirit
and they told the children
to move on and stop making
such a racket
but they were too late
as the evil of man
became a fire-spirit and he
began to burn it all
as if the gods told him
to and he did he burned
it all only to save
a true breath for himself
and he breathed in the
final breath
as I bit into the fruit
given to me by a fallen child
with wings made of the
sorrow of all the good spirits
and as I swallowed
I swallowed all of the flames
as

a

true

breath

saved

us.

A feather belonging

Came upon a place where
all the trains had stopped
and there were no sounds
coming from this city as the
hour changed and all
the god-fearing addicts
stepped out into the light
of an August moon as I sat
down and smoked a bit
and then quickly poked around
for a century old vein and
found it as the trains began
to move around me as my
liquid death took its time
to reach my everlasting
pleasure and then all the other
addicts looked up at the
August moon and they
prayed for death as I moved
on as I do and I am now
a demon as the poison
takes away any power
or gifts that I may have had
and I am walking into the walls
of this place where addicts die
from time to time and I could
heal all and myself
but the choice is not mine
and I knew that long ago
when I created the sun

and the August moon
as a feather of belonging
floats by me as I score again
and I slip into an alley that
smells like the warm desire
of piss and puke and I look
up one more time and see the
feather as it belongs to no one
and all the addicts close their eyes
as the August moon explodes
and the sun creeps forward from
the edge of this shit hole and all
the addicts look at me and they say:
please father
please let us go
and I close my eyes
and they all disappear
as the needle and the poison
penetrates all of me and what
is left of this sh:lam
the doctor
the demon
the unforgiving
as a feather
of belonging
dances
across
another
August
moon.

The pleasure of you

The people gathered and danced
for days and nights trying to
bring back a great woman
who had drowned trying to
reach the other side of the river
to save the children who had
all been given a sickness
from a faraway place
and this is where I first met
her
this sh:lam who did
not dance but she sat
in the back and she stared
at everyone but no one
looked into her eyes
for they knew of her power
and if you looked into her eyes
you would become frozen
and she could have all
of your being
and of course
the fool I am
the poisoned sh:lam
I am I looked into her eyes
and she took me away from the
gathering and we landed
beside a cedar tree
and she said: take me
and I did I stood behind her
and standing up I took her

and she looked back at me
and the fool I am I looked
into her eyes again and then
we were gone again and this
time we landed on a street
on the east side and we both
were begging for change
so we could kill the demon
that had taken both of us
and we drove those needles
into our arms over and over
again and when I looked
up I saw her eyes and we
were gone again into
the wind and we never
did land together as she
disappeared as the wind
caught her final words:
the pleasure of you
the
pleasure
of
you.

A blanket, a stone, a cigarette

When I walk into a new village the
children run up to me to touch
my hand and then they run away
in laughter as the old come to me
and they touch my hand and they
too run away in laughter as I
reach the life of the village
where the fire is kept
and I sit and I wait for the sick
to come to me and I touch them
upon the head and I rub my
hands together and touch them
as they get up and run around
the fire with laughter and tears
of joy for they have been healed
and the next sits down and I
continue until there is no one left
to heal and I get up and I walk on
and when I walk into a new city
the dreads and the dead come up
to me and they spit at me and tell
me to go back to hell and they
run away as I raise my hands
up to the dark sky and they all
fall into the cracks and holes
that the humans have built
for them as the ladies come
to me and they stand in perfect
form and they walk to me as
a great force of kindness and
I let them touch my hands

and they walk away
in a grand formation
and they attack the city
searching for the pain
and the pleasure of this city
as the tortured and the
unforgiven come to me
seeking a way out from
their afflictions and I let
them touch my hands and they
run away in search for one more
hit of paradise as they fall down
a deepening hole dug there by
the humans of this city
and when I am done
I walk to the ocean and I
dive in to cleanse myself
of all the blood and guts
of my torment as a sh:lam
and I come up with a stone
in my hand to the surface
for one more cigarette
and I let it burn as a young child
comes to me and covers me
in a blanket made of dreams
and I sit
as the world spins
out of control
for
another
moment
of
bliss.

A cup runneth over

I once attended a church
where snakes were passed
around and the believers kissed
them and threw them into the air
and as they fell the snakes would
look at me and I knew they were
taking away my powers so when
they threw the snakes into the air
I would spit fire at them and they
would explode into small bits
of belief and then the snake people
began their chant that had been
made up but they liked it and
they would shuffle to
the left and to the right
and grab another snake
from a box and throw it up
into the air and I tired
of spitting and left out the
back door and never looked
back for I knew the snakes
were trying to take from me
the one gift that I had always
had and that was forgiveness
and I walked on to another
church and the people there
were dressed in white robes
and they had the same made-up
chant as the last church
and they wore pointed hats

and they deemed all colour to be
the devil and when I walked in
they screamed at me to move on
or they would burn me on a cross
and send me back to hell
so I turned and walked out
the back door but this time
I looked back and met
their eyes and I forgave them
as the church exploded
and this caused the little
bits of heaven to mix with
the falling hatred and I walked
on as my cup runneth over
and I sat down and looked
across the world and all it was
were some churches standing
to the heavens
as others burned
in
the ashes
of
forgiveness.

I make the bend in the road

I have loved all the women I
have been with and they loved me as
much as I could allow them mostly
because I do not stay very long
in one place and I move and
I make the bend in the road
and I am a new man in another part
of history and today the leaves
have fallen and the rains have soaked
the dust of this dirt road and I knock
on her door and she lets me in and we
sit and talk about the moon and the
losses we both have suffered and
later when the red moon comes out
we are on her bed and I enter her
and she closes her eyes and she whispers
to me that I only love her and I do
as I am lost upon the moon and I
walk away and the bend in the road
disappears as I am in a new part
of history and there are no houses
only homes made of dirt and I enter
one of the doors and she is there
again another woman who talks
about the moon and her losses
and we sip tea and dream about tomorrow
as I undress and she takes me and she
destroys me and I walk away as the
road does not bend but I walk
to the very edge and a city
appears and I go into a house
and it is empty as the woman that

was here has been taken and they
could not find her but she is in
my dreams and I step into her
world for a moment to caress her
and comfort her as she begins her
steps into the other side of all this
and I kiss her and tell her I love her
and she smiles and says she knows
this and she tells me about the
moon when she was taken by
an evil man and she says
to me:
the moon was the red
of all the reds on earth
and it stopped the hurt
as this evil man
choked the life
out of me
and I came here
and I walked to this side
of history and I hoped
they will remember me
and I tell her they will
as I walk away and down
and make another bend in the road
and it joins the other
lost beautiful women of history
and all the bends join as if
they were the hands of women
and they caress me
as the
blood red
moon
rises.

I live at the corner of

This is the century of the
changing of seasons that I
have survived into and I am
alone because the world is a
safer place when I am hunting
the sacrifice that has to be made
and throughout my lives the ones
who most have to be sent forth
are men and I find them and I walk
up to them and they do not see me
as a healer but as someone
who will end their pain and
the pain they have done
to others so I quickly
snap their necks and leave them
on the sidewalk and I walk
away to the next man and he
pleads for me to let him go
but he has killed children
and the snap of his neck lessens
the tragedy of it and I walk
and then I rest a bit
in the corner of a fire-gutted
hotel that once housed all
the drunks and addicts and I sleep till
morning and walk on as the dragon
enters my blood and opens up
everything about me and who I am
and I walk and I see a man
who is waiting for me and I ask

him what he did in this life
and he tells me he was a
pig farmer and I snap his neck
as the dragon covers me in a
warm sense of
righteousness
and I walk on
and the clouds lift and the
sky opens up as the
sidewalks are covered
in neckless men who
in one way or another
took all our beauty
from this time
and another
century passes
as I
live
at the
corner
of
empathy
and
lust.

There they were

On a cliff I look down into
an unknown valley which for me
is different as I have
been across the earth a
thousand times and I have
climbed every tree and I have
swam all the oceans and I have
climbed the tallest mountains
that this planet has to offer and
as I look down I see an old friend
and he is walking slowly across
the horizon as his footsteps create
lakes and streams and the fish
come home once again repeating
their brilliant life and my friend
is gone but the wind picks up
his scent and they always tell
children that you will smell
the Sasquatch before you see
him and he is gone and I become
the eagle for a day and I take off
into the cold winds of the west
coast and I glide across the
thickness of the trees and I
hunger so I dive down and
take a fish and I devour it before
I have taken more than
is needed to fly to the valley
below and I land and I become
the bear and I am itchy so

I scratch myself against
a dead tree and the bugs
fall from me and they fly
out into the cold winds
and I crawl up into a hole
and I sleep for a generation
and when I wake up I have
become a human and I look
out into the warmth of a new day
and I am still itchy so I prick
my arms with a needle and
I become him again
yes I become the doctor
and there they were the whole time
sitting there watching me and they
the other sh:lams say to me:
you are back brother
stay with us awhile
and I do
as the pain fades and my eyes
open and I see
as far as I can see
and I see the glory
of my pain
as I scratch my body
until it bleeds
and the blood falls as
the footsteps
of the Sasquatch
fill with my blood
and tears
as I become empty

and I become
what I am
and that
is
a
forgotten
man.

Pray the good prayer

A gathering of men in black robes
brings together all the priests
of sainthood and there on the wall
a cross of another man
who supposedly died for
all the sins but he could
not heal these men as
each and every one had
done harm to a young boy
and that boy could no
longer feel and I was too late
to heal those boys and I could
only look on as they too hung
from the wall of a church and the
families gathered and cried and cried
but tears could not bring them back
and I was at that gathering where
the men in black robes all joined hands
and begged for forgiveness and I told
them to come to me and one by one
they came to me and I looked
into their eyes and I saw the same
distant evil of the past pleasures
where they tore away the innocence
of a young boy and I reached out
to each man in a black robe and as they
touched me they would slowly
fade into smoke and the
smoke rose up and formed
a cross on the wall and I

touched and forgave a
hundred men in black robes
and later I sat in that old church
and all the boys who used to
hang on the walls came and they
joined hands and sang a song so
old that there were no words
only the sounds of the fallen
and the smoke on the cross faded
back to where all of this had
come from and I sat there
for years listening to that song
over and over again and then
I stood up and walked out
and on to the next gathering
and in the distance I could hear
that song
as it became
a prayer
and
it
was the
good
prayer.

Tilt the answers

If the sun burned down
and all the animals slept and
the humans left for the summer
all there would be on this earth
would be the spirits and me
as I join them for a laugh
and some tears as we
reminisce about days gone by
and later I left and became
a ghost and all the earth was mine
to taste and take from and the
first thing I tasted was a sweet apple and then
I devoured an ocean of fish
and then I stalked and took some
wild meat that did not go to sleep
when they should have and I washed
it all down with a sea of love and then
I became a human and I am back
in time and I am still on the street
and they are looking for me
because somewhere along
the way I became known
for my healing powers and the
sick and the twisted came to me
and they sit quietly waiting their turn
and I heal them all and the taste
of illness forms a need to spit
so I do I spit a world of blood
onto the ground and wait a moment
and then I burn black the desire

and the drugs and I push it into me
and I am a human who heals the
tormented and the forgotten
and I walk the streets and I try
to find her but she is gone they say
and they say she delighted herself
one time too many and she is now
on the other side and she tilts
the answers and I ask a question
as the black tar takes me away
and I float above the spirits as they
kiss each other and wave to me
as I fall
and fall
to
a
place
I
never
knew.

A gun for you

Over time I have been asked
to come into a village and rid
them of the abusers and the
hatred and so I do I walk in
as the evil comes to me and they
laugh and say mean things and then
I reach out and they grab my hand
and they burst into flames and
then they turn to ice and they are
forgotten forever and then
I walk on always aware of the
mean things that are said to me
or about me and it hurts a bit
but then I give myself a taste of
freedom and I am away and
on a different road and about
to enter another village and the evil
comes at me with sticks and guns and they
shoot at me and miss and their sticks
just feed the fire they become when I
hold out my hands to them and they smile
as they turn into ice and are forgotten
and I take more of my desire as I am so far gone
that I need to rest and I find myself in
an alley of a big town and all the brothers
and sisters are there and they come to me
and hold out their hands begging me to end
it for them and I do I try my best to send
them back to fire and ice and to be
really forgotten and then I sleep and

I dream about all of this and when I
awake I am on an island and all the
dogs are barking at me and they snarl
and wag their tails and they run away
as I reach out to them and it is then
that I find her and she has been here
all this time and she is the beauty
of all beauty and I reach for her and she
reaches for me and the touch of our
hands explodes into our love
for the other and the dogs bark
as there is a loud noise in the distance
and it is of a gunshot as another
brother or sister has ended their
life as I swim in my desire
for the one I love but she too
explodes into fire and ice
as the dogs bark and form
the words:
this
gun
is
for
you.

A strand of red cedar

I dove into the cold river
and I swam upstream and
walked out and was met by
children who were sniffing
gasoline and they looked right
through me and they began to giggle
and sniff more until they could not
see me anymore and I walked
back to the river and for the
children I left a strand of red cedar
and then I jumped back into
the cold river and I swam downstream
and reached the ocean and was met
by a people in giant canoes and all
of them had smallpox and they
had been sent away by their people
and on the ocean they died one by one
and as I swam by them I tossed
a strand of red cedar and it made them
disappear in the mist of suffering
and I swam until I reached a rocky
cliff and I climbed out and I was
met by more children who had
been taken by the church of god
and they were told to stand
on the edge of this cliff and repent
their sins and god would answer them
and they too disappeared into the mist
as I tossed another strand of red cedar
and I dove back into the ocean and

swam all the way to another coast
of this planet and I walked
out and met the world
as it spun and spun
out of control and all
the people were rushing
here and there and the air
was putrid and the children
came to me and they all asked
for a way out from the poison
that stuck into their blood
and I tossed a strand of red cedar
as the
poison
took all of them
and me
in a
vicious
silence.

I can see her halo

Went to the sky and the winds
took me away far from all
of my own pain and anguish
and the angels came to me and sang
a song or two and then they
were gone and then I could hear
the sounds of animals who were
tearing to pieces one of
their own and you could hear
the screams as it died and then
I fell from the sky but was ok
as I landed softly and I looked
across the treeline and I could
see her halo and I chased after
her
this beauty
this demon
this angel of no one for no one
and I chased and caught her
and we made noises like
the animals as we tore into the other
and later we slept and I had a dream
of a much quieter existence but that
was just a dream and I gave myself
to her again and she wept
and I wept and we wept angel tears
and I can still see her halo as she went back
up the mountain where her kind lived
and they sang songs for her return
and I was left alone as I have been

for ten thousand years and I needed
a taste of acceptance and I searched
and searched and found it and I let
it attack me and the sounds of animals
as they devoured one of their own
entered into me and I tried to get up
into the sky but I could not
and then the earth surrounded me
and took me under and I stayed there
for another ten thousand years
and when I came up for a breath
of air I could faintly
in the distance
I could
see
her
halo.

Translated loosely

The gods took one look at me
and they laughed and said goodbye
as the light from the center of the earth
erupted and the smoke and fire
burned all that stood in its way
and then the fire entered my hands
and that is how I was given one
of my gifts and I threw the flames
at the deviant and the desolate
of this time and then it all
settled down and I found myself
in a bar on the east side of nothingness
and I sipped rum and coke and snorted
a line and the ladies from the street came over
to my table and told me that you
had been looking for me and that I was
the chosen one for the masses and it was
the flames in my hands and the words
that I spoke that could save the dreads
and derelicts of this city and that I could
rise up and heal the wounds that have
festered for far too long so I rise up
and I throw all of my fire at the stink
and piss and misery and then you enter
the bar and we dance to an old song sung
by all the ladies of the street and then the
song is joined by a thousand drummers
and they pound their drums
as the fire burns outside of this bar
and it engulfs the stink and piss

and misery and we dance and dance
and we kiss and as our tongues touch we
are thrown into a wind that takes us
even higher above the treacherous day
and we dance and we dance as the
ladies of the street sing the old song
and the drummers pound their drums
and all is healed for now as my lover
and I dance the dance and when it
is over
the bar becomes quiet
and all
you can hear
are the
whispers
of
the
lost.

How do we fall apart?

One thousand years ago I found
myself on the river and I stood
between two river tribes and they
were about to go to war against
each other so I said a few words
and I held up my hands and then
they attacked each other with
gallant clubs and knives made
of stone and they ripped each
other apart like animals at a
winter feast and they clubbed
each other in the head and some
who could not escape were buried
up to their necks in the sands of the bank
of the bloody river and they looked at me
but I had already raised my hands and said
a few words and as the clubs smashed
their heads in they closed their eyes
and asked the question:
how do we fall apart?
I rose up
walked away from
this pain and loss and it became quiet
as the war was over and peace came
and the sun came out
and the fish came back
and all the people feasted upon
the first fish laughing like
animals at a winter's feast and I sat
down and raised my hands and said

a few words and the people came to me
and they touched my hands as the war was over
and we all knew that we had fallen apart
and the juices burned in the fire as the fish
was cooked and the sun came out
and as I raised my hands up
all the flowers of the world opened up
and forgave them
these people of war and peace
and I closed my eyes
as a single tear fell
to the sands
of the bank
of this
lovely
bloody
river.

Posed

We lay there in a statuesque
embrace holding on as if we
are spinning out of control
as if we fell from the sky
and landed together in a
beautiful symbol of embrace
of love but we hate the faith
we have chosen and the devil
and the dragon kiss us every waking
minute of our days and nights
and the pain in our heads escapes
a bit after each taste of this drug
while we drool before each cut it
takes to put into our spirits
and we are away into the evening
of a very quiet city night as the
people are all out for a night of
panic and we lay in our embrace
and I love her and she loves me
and we finally wake up and
I remember who I am and where
I came from and I think it was up
river but I cannot be sure as
I look at myself and I am
a shade darker than I was before
and I look at her and she is nothing
more than the bones of a girl I once
knew and when there were children
we had once but they have been taken
and cared for by the people who are

spending a quiet night in the
safety of a warm home up
river somewhere
and I look at myself
and I realize that the dragon
has taken over me and my
mind and I am faltering
and I am standing here
but you know what
I am here as if a great spirit
from up there
has gently
placed me here
in
this
diabolical
pose.

When the curious

At a gathering of fools they wept
and wept until daylight and then the
fire went out and everyone went home
to the insane streets of the pathetic
city where gloom and odour roam
around like an untied balloon as it
floats up into the darkness and the
street comes alive and the people
gather and steal and rob each other
for a bit of coin to buy a piece of
blackness that when burned becomes
the liquid devil that we all dream of
and I am there robbing and stealing
for a lick of the spoon and when I am
satisfied I float up like the untied
balloon and I watch the gathering
of the people as they wept and wept
and I climb higher and I am gone
and the only way back is when my
blood mixes with the liquid in my arm
and that is the only time I am real and the
only time I am unreal and I want
to heal them like I am healed but
when I try they all scatter
and hide in the corners of this
place where a healer like me
has very little power to even
heal himself so I float above
myself and when I look down
I see myself convulsing and kicking

and scratching at my arms as if
being attacked by a million spiders
and they overtake me and I am
gone but not really gone
as I am the fate
of my addiction
and I am gifted with
the gift of healing
and when I try and heal myself
I fail as I float too far
over and when I look down
I am gone as the last spider
crawls to the corner
and this is where
the curious
wept for
me.

How do you fall?

Come to me my lovely woman
with all of your thorns and metal
daggers ready to stick me and
love me like you do
yes you perfect human with your
kisses and your touches caressing
me when I am in a frenzy of
uncontrollable need to fix
this trauma of who I am and you
always know the words to throw
into my ears when I am too high
to come down and caress you
like the dream you are
and I remember your strength
and I remember your long legs
wrapped around me telling me
to keep pushing lover keep
pushing into me and never
let go so I keep pushing until
the darkness comes back
and I am all alone as if you
were never there
no you were taken like the
rest of them
taken away too soon from me
and the gifts given to me
I could have helped
I would have kept you
hidden but those men
those killers of women

found you on a highway
and I was too far gone
on a binge of some powder
that tasted better than
our first kiss and now all
I have of her is her passion
this angel of the streets
and I am all alone with
only a fragment of you
only a piece of your heart
joins mine and I pray
for the release but I am
to be born again
as if in solitude
is my consequence
of what I love and indulge
in this poor poor man's
choice
of
how
do
you
fall.

The tear of you

Up river an old sh:lam stood
up and his eyes were covered
and he spoke to the people
and he scolded them for not
following the teachings and the
people listened and the old
sh:lam spoke well into
the next morning and as the
sun rose up the fire was still
burning and all the people
had left and the only one left
was the sh:lam and he kept the
fire going and the sun turned
into the moon and I am
walking as fast as I can to save
a brother who is slowly dying
and when I reach him he
is already gone and standing
beside him is the old sh:lam
and he picks up the brother
of ours and they both enter
the other side and I am left there
all alone and so I start a fire and stare
into the smoke and the visions
I see are of that brother's life
on the streets and all his worries
are gone and I see him in his
village and all the people have gathered
around a great fire and the smoke rises up
and everyone welcomes home

the brother and the people
cry the tear of you brother
please have peace as you
are no longer on the streets
but you are home and the fire
burned into the night and the sun
came out and all the people had left
and the only one there was
the old sh:lam
his eyes
still
covered.

The correction

They put my bones in a
cedar box at the top of the
tallest tree along the deepest
part of this cold river and when I
appear again I am in the form
of a raven and I take off up high
into the mountains and when I
land I become a sh:lam again
and I am so pure with the gift
of healing that I would just
look at the sick and they would
be cured of any dreaded disease
brought up river by men who
wished to end the people and so
I looked at these men too and
they fell sick with starvation and
could not understand that the
river was full of fish because all
they desired was a piece of gold
for their prayers but they floated
away back down river as nothing
more than the shell of a man that
they used to be and when I walked
further away from them I learned
too that I could control time and I
changed it to the present and our
people have left their village and they
left the fish and they hunted the cities
for a taste of gold and the power of it
that could take away their losses and

they drift around the streets as shells
of who they were and I look at them
and they float away back to the river
and they become fish and they swim
upriver to their old villages and they
become a human again and they have
been cleansed of their sickness and despair
of that golden dream and I look away
and walk into the distant future and
I am here sitting upon the tallest
mountain made of gold as the sun
causes it to shimmer and light the
world
as the
correction
has
been
made.

Speak to the rains

When they took the children
by trains and the boats and settled
them in for their first night away
from home for an eternity those
children did not sleep for fear of
closing their eyes would awake the
demons that this new home had in
the basement and the corners where
the sudden movement caused one child
to cry for his momma but momma was
long gone into a bottle of glass that was
later smashed and the pieces were used
to cut away the pain that all the
children had woven deep into their
minds and in the morning they were
given a bowl of cold nothing and it
tasted like the corners of this place
and the children were told to strip
and they were washed with
cold water and they were told that
this new god would carry them
to a far place up in the heavens
and the children did not make a sound
and they did not cry out for fear of
the man in the corner who stood there
with a thick black belt and he would
hit a child who cried and the children
became tough and would not show
fear and this angered the man in the
corner and he would hit them anyways

and this is when I showed up because
I had seen this before and I took
that man with the black belt and
grabbed him by the throat until all
of his holy sacred air left his body
and then I threw him into a fire I
had built just for him and he wailed
like a child as the hell I gave him
took all of him and the children
rose up and they told one another
to speak to the rains and that a sh:lam
would come and I did over and over
again I took the bad men
into the corners
as
if
god
told
me
to.

Look good in a cage

As the rains fall I am on a boat
drifting down river and on the shore
I see three women sh:lams and they are
laughing at me and then they begin to
stir the wind and the river erupts
into waves and rocks my boat from
side to side and I lift the boat up into
the air and I fly away from their
laughter and then the world calms
and I see yet another sh:lam a man
who sees me and my boat and
he laughs and then turns the river
to ice and I am frozen in one spot
so I dive out of the boat and into
the ice and I go under
and I swim for days until
I reach the warmth of the ocean
and I am free of their powers
but then a great whale comes up
beside me and looks into my eyes
and I know this whale and he
swallows me and I fall down
into his belly and I am trapped
until I rub my hands together
and then the whale opens his
great mouth and I am free and I
walk out of the ocean and I am
on an island and all the animals
come to me and say to me that I
would look good in a cage and they

laugh as I rub my hands together
and the flames and smoke frightens
the animals away and I am finally
at peace and alone so I make a fire
and dance around the flames and smoke
and this is where I come to terms
with who I am and what I am to do
for the world and then I lay down
and sleep and the dreams come
and I have seen them before as they
are the dreams of
wind
and ice
and the eternal mouth
of a great whale
that
swallows me
over
and
over
and
over.

Close to the flatness

When all the clocks stopped
I awoke sweating and unable
to remember who I was and looked
around the garbage that I had slept
in and I did not recognize this room
and how I had ended up here
or where my shoes were and again
who I was seemed to be forgotten
so I got up and went out into
the streets and there I began
to come about and I recognized
all the poor and hungry and I
recognized all the dogs as they
barked at me telling me to
behave so I did and I kept
walking and found her
she was waiting for me and we
both took a taste of the other
and that mixed with what was
left of our blood and we soared
high into the calmness of the
night's sky and we flew around
for hours as the dogs barked
at me and called me a liar for I
had not behaved but I tried
to tell them that most of
my mind was gone as was my
blood but me and my girl
would fly above the treachery
of this city and we flew between

the buildings and all the poor people
looked up at us and waited for what
happened every night and yes
they waited for me and my girl
to fall and I did I fell as if I had
no wings at all and I fell back
onto the garbage from the night
before and I was close to the
flatness of this earth and I could
not remember who I was and my
girl was gone because she was never
there in the first place and I stayed
there trying to remember who I was
and where did all my blood go and
then I remembered that I was not
an angel no I was a liar
as the dogs barked
in agreement
and their sound was
so beautiful
that
it
could've
been
a
song.

About the cross

In the river flowing downstream
bathing myself of all my sins and it
feels good this mountain fed river and
my spirit sings and my song carries on
into the forest and the people come
to the shore and they stare at me hoping
I will swim to them and heal them but
I keep going and I come to the end of the river
and I get out and I am naked and there is
a gathering of black robes and they are
chanting a song to Jesus and they see me
and begin to scream that I am the devil
and I have to run into the forest and I make
my clothes out of cedar and I make a big hat
and it covers my eyes and I walk back out
and the black robes are gone but they have
left a cross and there is a man nailed
to it and so I build myself a cross and I
nail myself beside this man but he has
already gone and they say he woke up
three days later and that men in black
robes eat his body and drink his blood
in ceremony and I stayed there on that
cross for centuries and then
I climbed down and stripped
and went into the river but this
time I swam up river and all along
the shore the people made fires
and sang songs to me as if I was some
sort of saviour but I wanted to tell them

that I am just a sh:lam a doctor who is
lost and I am searching for my love and I
keep swimming as the songs and the fires
fade and I am back up in the mountains
and the snow melts and flows into the river
and I strip again and jump back in and I
swim back down and I see the holes in
my hands and feet and I am still wearing
that big hat
made
of
thorns.